Rookie
Read-About® Health

Dairy

By Susan DerKazarian

Consultants

Reading Adviser
Nanci R. Vargus, EdD
Assistant Professor of Literacy
University of Indianapolis, Indianapolis, Indiana

Subject Adviser
Janet M. Gilchrist, PhD, RD
Nutritionist

Children's Press®
A Division of Scholastic Inc.
New York   Toronto   London   Auckland   Sydney
Mexico City   New Delhi   Hong Kong
Danbury, Connecticut

Designer: Herman Adler Design
Photo Researcher: Caroline Anderson
The photo on the cover shows different sources of dairy.

Library of Congress Cataloging-in-Publication Data

DerKazarian, Susan, 1969–
  Dairy / by Susan DerKazarian.
    p. cm. — (Rookie read-about health)
  Includes index.
  ISBN 0-516-23672-5 (lib. bdg.)   0-516-25925-3 (pbk.)
  1. Dairy products—Juvenile literature. I. Title. II. Series.
  TX377.D47 2005
  641.3'7—dc22   2005004634

1 2 3 4 5 6 7 8 9 10 R 14 13 12 11 10 09 08 07 06 05

Did you know that the milk you drank today was once inside a cow?

Milk is a dairy food. So are cheese, yogurt, and ice cream. They are all made from milk.

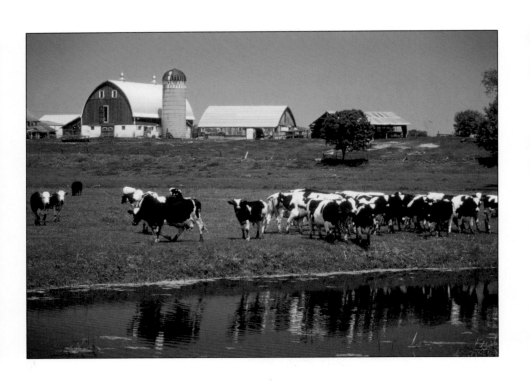

How does the milk get from the cow to you?

It all starts on a dairy farm. Cows live on these farms. Some farmers make dairy foods there.

A dairy farmer milks the cows every day. On small farms, this is sometimes done by hand. On larger farms, machines do this job.

A worker handles wheels of cheese at a plant.

Some of the milk is kept as milk. Some is shipped to plants. There it is made into cheese, yogurt, or other dairy foods.

Big trucks take the dairy foods from farms and plants and bring them to stores.

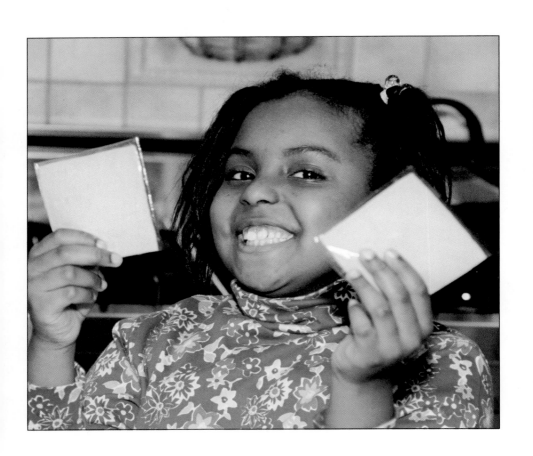

It is important to eat and drink dairy foods every day.

Dairy foods have many nutrients. You need nutrients to stay healthy.

Calcium is just one nutrient found in dairy foods. Calcium helps your bones grow and stay strong.

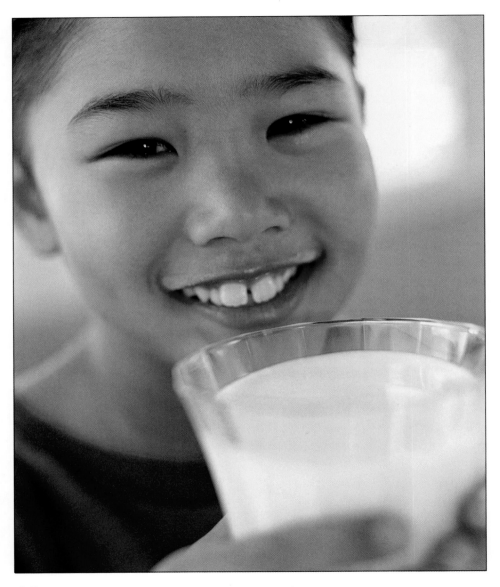

Calcium also helps keep your teeth strong and healthy.

Scientists came up with the Food Guidance System. It tells you how many times a day you should eat different types of food to stay healthy.

MyPyramid.gov
STEPS TO A HEALTHIER YOU

Grain Group
Make half your grains whole

Vegetable Group
Vary your veggies

Fruit Group
Focus on fruits

Milk Group
Get your calcium-rich foods

Meat & Bean Group
Go lean with protein

21

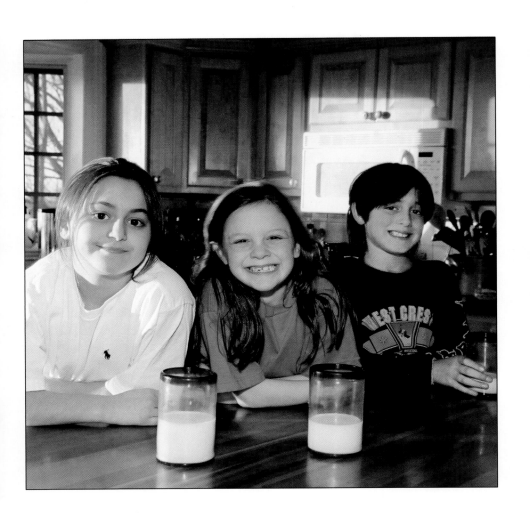

The Food Guidance System says we should eat two to three cups of dairy foods every day.

This is easy to do. You can enjoy a few slices of cheese, a cup of yogurt, and a glass of milk.

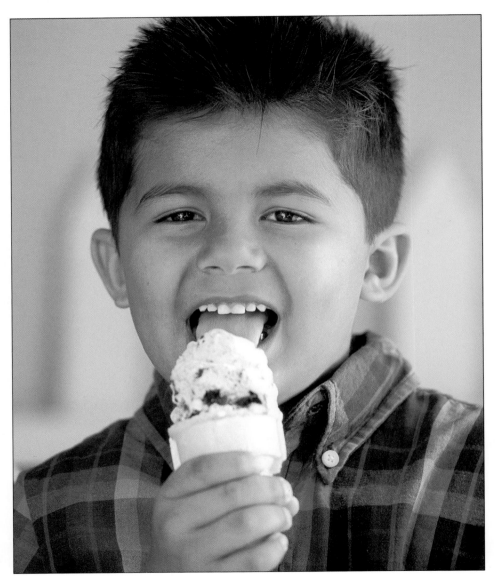

Once in a while, a small bowl of ice cream or pudding makes a tasty dairy treat. Yum!

Dairy foods taste good. They are also good for you. Remember to eat them every day!

Words You Know

bones

cheese

cow

farm

ice cream

milk

teeth

yogurt

Index

About the Author

Susan DerKazarian is senior editor at Mondo Publishing in New York City, where she helps publish books for children. In her spare time, Susan enjoys writing children's books, reading, going to the beach, and hiking.

Photo Credits

Photographs © 2005: Corbis Images: 9 (Paul Gun), 5 top left, 30 top right (Spencer Jones/PictureArts); Dembinsky Photo Association/Richard Hamilton Smith: 6, 30 bottom right; Envision Stock Photography Inc.: 3, 30 bottom left (Deborah Burke), cover (Steven Mark Needham); Getty Images/Brand X Pictures: 5, 31 top right; Peter Arnold, Inc./Alex Grey: 17, 30 top left; PhotoEdit: 5 bottom, 31 top left (Rachel Epstein), 26 (David Young-Wolff); Phototake, Inc./Maximilian Stock LTD: 10; PictureQuest/Maximilian: 5 top right, 31 bottom right; Randy Matusow: 14, 22, 25, 29; Robertstock.com./Bananastock Ltd.: 18, 31 bottom left; U.S. Department of Agriculture/Ken Hammond: 13.